KINGDOM CULTURE

THE SERMON ON THE MOUNT

tara beth leach

KINGDOM CULTURE
THE SERMON ON THE MOUNT

workbook

BEACON HILL PRESS
OF KANSAS CITY

Copyright © 2017 by Beacon Hill Press of Kansas City
Beacon Hill Press of Kansas City
PO Box 419527
Kansas City, MO 64141
www.beaconhillbooks.com
978-0-8341-3616-8

Printed in the
United States of America

Cover Design: J.R. Caines
Interior Design: Sharon Page

The internet addresses, email addresses, and phone numbers in this book are accurate at the time of publication. They are provided as a resource. Beacon Hill Press does not endorse them or vouch for their content or permanence.

This Bible study was inspired and influenced by Scot McKnight's *The Story of God Bible Commentary: Sermon on the Mount* (Grand Rapids: Zondervan, 2013). Referenced with permission of the author.

10 9 8 7 6 5 4 3 2 1

CONTENTS

Welcome 7

Session 1: The Sermon on the Mount 8
{Matthew 5:1–2; 7:24—8:1}

Session 2: The Beatitudes 11
{Matthew 5:3–12}

Session 3: Salt and Light 27
{Matthew 5:13–16}

Session 4: Jesus Is the Fulfillment of the Law 41
{Matthew 5:17–32}

Session 5: Love Your Enemies 61
{Matthew 5:33–48}

Session 6: Prayer and Fasting 77
{Matthew 6:1–18}

Session 7: Judgment and Discernment 95
{Matthew 6:19—7:12}

Session 8: Discipleship and the Wise & Foolish Builders 119
{Matthew 7:13–27}

WELCOME

We are so glad you have chosen to participate in the *Kingdom Culture: The Sermon on the Mount* video-series study! This book is yours to work through privately or cooperatively with others as you desire. Each session, with the exception of Session 1, contains four days' worth of material to work through in the week (or weeks) leading up to your group meeting, where you will watch the video that corresponds with that session.

Tara Beth has designed this workbook to be both as engaging and as challenging as possible for you, the participant, in the days between when your group meets. In each session's set of content, there are questions, Bible readings, teachings, and practices to consider that will prepare you for the next video teaching. We recommend working through each day of content at your own pace *before* viewing the corresponding video with your group. Some of the questions will be easy to answer, and some may not be so easy. Some may stump you until after you've viewed the appropriate video. That's okay.

We do encourage you to bring your workbook along to your group meetings so that you can fill in any holes left during the week or take notes during the video teachings (there is space provided at the end of each session for note-taking purposes).

We hope and pray that this study will challenge, invigorate, and transform the way you see yourself as a disciple of Christ. God's blessing be upon you as you and your small group begin this journey through the Sermon on the Mount.

THE SERMON ON THE MOUNT

Learn the Story
Video Teaching Notes

This space is for you to take notes while watching *Kingdom Culture* "Session 1 // The Sermon on the Mount." You can refer to these notes later, if needed, while working through the rest of the workbook.

Matthew 5:1–2
Matthew 7:24—8:1

"Now when Jesus saw the crowds, he went up on a mountainside and sat down. His disciples came to him, and he began to teach them."
—Matthew 5:1–2

THE BEATITUDES

Read the Story

Matthew 5:3–12

[3] "Blessed are the poor in spirit,

for theirs is the kingdom of heaven.

[4] Blessed are those who mourn,

for they will be comforted.

[5] Blessed are the meek,

for they will inherit the earth.

[6] Blessed are those who hunger and thirst for righteousness,

for they will be filled.

[7] Blessed are the merciful,

for they will be shown mercy.

[8] Blessed are the pure in heart,

for they will see God.

[9] Blessed are the peacemakers,

for they will be called children of God.

[10] Blessed are those who are persecuted because of righteousness,

for theirs is the kingdom of heaven.

[11] "Blessed are you when people insult you, persecute you and falsely say all kinds of evil against you because of me. [12] Rejoice and be glad, because great is your reward in heaven, for in the same way they persecuted the prophets who were before you."

Study the Story

Read Matthew 5:1 and note where Jesus goes.

Read the following passages and note where Moses goes in each one.

Exodus 24:12–13

Exodus 34:1–4

Deuteronomy 9:9

Deuteronomy 10:3

Mountainside scenes occur often throughout the Old Testament, especially with Moses.

What are the similarities and differences between the people to whom Moses gives the law and the people to whom Jesus preaches the Sermon on the Mount?

What are the similarities and differences between Moses and Jesus?

Read the following passages and note the common thread about Jesus.

Matthew 7:28–29	Matthew 19:16
Matthew 8:19	Matthew 22:16
Matthew 9:11	Matthew 22:24
Matthew 12:38	Matthew 22:36
Matthew 17:24	Matthew 26:18

If you had to pick one word that perfectly describes Jesus based on the passages you just read, what word would it be?

What type of posture, then, are we to have while reading the Sermon on the Mount?

In 2010 I began my seminary journey with Northern Baptist Theological Seminary. I had Bible classes in undergrad and had been in full-time, pastoral ministry for six years, but I knew it was time to go back to school. With a nine-month-old at home and another baby on the way, I just wanted to get through school—to survive. I confess: My attitude wasn't the greatest. I had already been a student of the Bible, I had practical ministry experience, and I just wanted the degree. I approached my first few classes with arrogance and impatience. Each class, I hurried in and hurried back out without truly soaking in the words of my professors.

My first summer at Northern, I enrolled in a week-long module on the book of Revelation, taught by Dr. Gerald Borchert. After I walked into the classroom and took my seat, a man who looked to be around the age of eighty slowly walked into the room and sat down at the front. I slumped in my chair and thought, *This is going to be a long and boring week; bring on the caffeine.*

Dr. Borchert sat down, opened his Bible, and began to read the opening words to the book of Revelation and the vision of Christ so majestically illustrated by John. Then he began to teach in a way I had never been taught from the Bible. His words penetrated, convicted, and carried authority. Eight hours of teaching evaporated in seemingly a moment. The next day I arrived at class, rushed to the first row, and found myself sitting on the edge of my chair while hanging on every word. For the first time in seminary, I took on the posture of a true student. I cared about every word Dr. Borchert had to say. I was hungry for more. I was open to learning new things, and, most of all, I allowed the words to form my heart, mind, and soul.

Over the next several weeks, you can approach this study with many different postures. You can approach as an expert, reading your own agenda into the text, or you can come as an open, surrendered, and humble student. Jesus is the teacher who even today calls his students to a radical life of surrendered obedience.

"Jesus is the teacher who even today calls his students to a radical life of surrendered obedience."

What can you do during this study to take on the posture of a student? Maybe you need to pray for the Spirit to humble you. Maybe you need to intentionally remove any distractions that could hinder you from taking on this posture. Maybe it's as simple as whispering a daily prayer of surrender to our King and Savior, Jesus.

Write a prayer to God about how you desire to take on the posture of a student during this study. Don't be afraid to be honest—God's heard it all! Pray that God's Spirit would guide, teach, and lead your heart, mind, soul, and body during this study.

Study the Story

Read Matthew 5:1–12.

───────

My parents have called me a fish since the age of five. I loved the water, and I swam every chance I had, so my parents put me on a swim team. I excelled at swimming rather quickly; it was my sport.

But when I reached the eighth grade, none of the cool girls were swimmers—they were volleyball players. Every morning before the bell rang, most of the school gathered in the bleachers to watch the eighth-grade volleyball team practice their bump, set, spike routine. A few of the girls spiked the ball so hard that it slammed on the wall at the opposite end of the gym. The student audience always erupted with *ooohs* and *aaaahs*, and I sat there wishing I were one of the players.

When freshman year rolled around, I decided it was time to give this volleyball thing a go. The problem was, the only experience I had with volleyball was in gym class and the occasional passing of a ball back and forth with a neighborhood friend. So it shouldn't have been such a crushing surprise not to see my name on the team list at the end of tryouts.

I didn't make it. Of course not. I was among the least likely.

At the beginning of Jesus's Sermon on the Mount, he declares a list of the "in" group. Much like how I stood in the locker room looking for my name on the volleyball team list, many of Jesus's listeners hang on every word he says, whispering to themselves, "Did I make the list? Am I in or out? Whom is he talking about?"

Scot McKnight describes the purpose of lists in the time of Jesus: "Listings like [the Beatitudes] . . . had two basic orientations: One list rolled out the names of saints, usually describing their behaviors, while another list focused on the characteristics of those who were observant of Torah and approved by God."*

To begin the Sermon on the Mount, Jesus does the most *unexpected* thing. He completely reverses the practice and names the least likely of people. Instead of naming the super-religious or the most faithful observers of Old Testament law, Jesus instead declares the

───────

*Scot McKnight, *The Story of God Bible Commentary: Sermon on the Mount* (Grand Rapids: Zondervan, 2013), 30.

blessed to be the marginalized who follow God even in the darkest of valleys. Jesus's reversal disrupts what the people of God believe to be the "in" group and invites them to imagine a different world.

Read Matthew 5:3–10 again. List below those whom Jesus says are blessed.

Blessed are . . .

1. Poor In Spirit

2. Those who mourn

3. The meek

4. Those who hunger and thirst for righteousness

5. The merciful

6. The pure in heart

7. The peacemakers

8. Those who are persecuted because of righteousness

Jesus boldly declares that this rugged, rag-tag group of people will populate the kingdom of God. The gospel of Luke also has a shortened version of the Beatitudes (6:20–23). In this version, though, Jesus also includes the woe statements. Read Luke 6:20–26 and note the differences you observe between the two lists.

1. The poor – when you've lost it all

2. The hungry –

3. Those who weep

4. Those who are hated, ostracized, insulted, & scorn

When you look at the differences between the Beatitudes and the woes, what kind of picture begins to form of the kingdom of God?

The Beatitudes are for people who are the least likely to succeed, the least likely to be chosen, the last in line, and clearly the weakest. Among the community of Jesus's listeners are people who are poor, people on the outside, people who are unclean and the least likely to earn a place in the kingdom. But Jesus audaciously includes and invites them into fellowship. This list includes people who love God in the midst of hunger, hardship, poverty, and oppression. Think for a moment of an example of someone you know who stuck with God even during valley moments. What is this person's character like? How did this person embody love for God?

Think for a moment about how you measure the "in" crowd. Piety? Frequency of church attendance? Faithful tithing? Outward appearance? Value system? Those who can memorize Bible verses or have showy spiritual gifts? Those who talk often about praying?

What do you notice about the inner qualities Jesus values? Reread Matthew 5:3–10 one more time. After reading, write below in your own words whom you understand the Beatitudes to be for today:

As we can see, the Beatitudes are not entrance requirements. They are not a list of virtues. When we take a step back for a moment, we see a King who invites all the *wrong people* to the table and into his presence, and Jesus does this in an intensely exclusive religious environment. Think for a moment about your local church. Are there groups of people who are—whether purposely or inadvertently—excluded from the fellowship? If so, who are they? Write a prayer below that the Spirit would help your local church be one that welcomes everyone.

Study the Story

Christians love to use the word *blessed*.

"Oh, what a *blessing* that you got the job you wanted!"
"You are so *blessed* to be able to stay at home with your children!"
"We have been really *blessed* financially."

I'm sure you've heard something along these lines too. Most often, we equate the word *blessed* with the happiness in our lives that results from things going according to our own plans and desires. But a rereading of the Matthew 5 text shows that blessings in the way Jesus talks about them are very different from the way we understand them today.

Read Matthew 5:3–10 one final time. After reflecting on the Beatitudes a little more, what would you conclude about the relationship between blessing and happiness?

Below, write which Beatitudes are most closely connected to one's relationship with God. Then write which ones are most closely connected to relationships with others.

Relationship with God:

Relationships with others:

We can safely conclude, then, that people who are blessed love God and love other people. Think of someone in your life who embodies loving God and loving others. Describe who this person is and how this person's life embodies these characteristics.

Live the Story

The apostle Paul commands Christians to "pray without ceasing" (1 Thessalonians 5:17, NRSV). Prayer can have many different postures. I sometimes pray on my knees; other times I pray while I'm out on a long run. Sometimes I even pray under my breath while in a crowd of people or in the middle of a tough meeting.

One of my favorite ways to pray is to go on a prayer walk. A prayer walk means praying on location. When I was in high school, I had a longing to see my fellow classmates turn their hearts to Jesus. So I made the commitment to walk around my high school thirty days in a row and pray for the Spirit to break down barriers, soften hearts, and turn lives to King Jesus. Prayer walks can be in our neighborhoods, in a mall, around a school, around or through a church—anywhere that we want to ask God to be present. A prayer walk is just another practice or posture of prayer.

Invite God to join you wherever you decide to pray.

Today, take a few moments to go on a prayer walk and pray for the people associated with that location. Maybe take a stroll through your neighborhood and pray that God would make you a better neighbor. Or perhaps you have a neighbor whom you know is going through a difficult time; as you walk by that house, pray for God's guidance, peace, and comfort to surround the household. Maybe the location for your prayer walk needs to be your or your spouse's workplace, or your child's school, or a local civic or government building. Own this exercise and invite God to join you wherever you decide to pray.

Learn the Story
Video Teaching Notes

Pray without ceasing.

SALT AND LIGHT

Read the Story

Matthew 5:13–16

¹³ "You are the salt of the earth. But if the salt loses its saltiness, how can it be made salty again? It is no longer good for anything, except to be thrown out and trampled underfoot.

¹⁴ "You are the light of the world. A town built on a hill cannot be hidden. ¹⁵ Neither do people light a lamp and put it under a bowl. Instead they put it on its stand, and it gives light to everyone in the house. ¹⁶ In the same way, let your light shine before others, that they may see your good deeds and glorify your Father in heaven."

Study the Story

Often while reading a particular text in the Bible, the inclination is to read with the goal of answering the question *What does this passage of Scripture mean to me?* While there are times in our lives when we may need to know the answer to that question, we can miss out on the Bible's grand narrative if that is the only question we ever ask ourselves when reading Scripture. Few scriptures are meant to be read in isolation because there is often a bigger story connecting scriptures to each other, from Genesis to Revelation. Listeners of Jesus's words in the Gospels would've noticed Old Testament nuances and connections that maybe we, as modern-day readers, don't always recognize.

Let's take a look at a handful of Old Testament passages that discuss salt in a literal sense to better understand the salt metaphor in Matthew 5:13.

Read the following passages and answer this question for each one: What is the purpose of salt in this passage?

Exodus 30:34–36

Leviticus 2:13

Job 6:6–7

In the New Testament, salt takes on a more metaphorical meaning for the purpose of teaching the followers of Jesus something important. Read the following passages and answer this question for each one: What is the purpose of the salt metaphor in this passage as it relates to the character of a disciple of Jesus?

Mark 9:49–50

Luke 14:34–35

Colossians 4:6

Salt was an essential ingredient for everyday life in biblical times, which is hard for us to imagine today because doctors and health professionals have advised we go easy on our salt intake. Today salt is more of an optional, less-is-more type of ingredient. If we understand salt as both essential and as an ingredient that can easily be overused, how does our view change of a disciple's role in the world?

Salt does not exist for its own sake; rather, salt functions as an ingredient to make something else better. With this function in mind, how does our view change of a disciple's role in the world?

Consider for a few moments (and take your time—be still!) the salt metaphor in Matthew 5:13 as well as the Beatitudes in Matthew 5:3–10. What images and themes come to mind? Ask the Spirit to reveal to you what particular qualities might be lacking in your own life. In the space below, write out a prayer for transformation. Pray that the Spirit would empower you to live a salty life and for the characteristics of Jesus to emerge in your life.

Study the Story

Read Matthew 5:13. What might make us uncomfortable about this verse?

It's hard to read this verse and not skip right over the second half and move on to verse 14. Verse 13 contains a powerful warning for listeners and disciples: If a disciple loses his or her saltiness, the disciple is no longer good for anything. Yikes. Some wonder if Jesus *really means* what he says when he says things like this that are hard. He is, after all, loving and gracious and kind. But this image of being thrown away as a consequence is used throughout Scripture and especially in Matthew. Read the following verses and note their similar sentiments:

Matthew 3:10
Matthew 5:29
Matthew 5:30
Matthew 7:19
Matthew 13:50
Matthew 18:8
Matthew 18:9

Jesus's warning pushes the disciple to recognize the danger of an ineffective witness. A Christian who does not live the kingdom lifestyle portrayed in the teachings of Jesus is worth as much as tasteless salt.

In one sitting, read the Sermon on the Mount all the way through (Matthew 5—7). As you read, take note of the character and actions of a salty disciple, *and* take note of the character and actions of a disciple who has lost his or her saltiness. Make two lists.

The character and actions of a salty disciple:

The character and actions of a disciple who has lost his or her saltiness:

A study like this can easily evoke a certain fear of life after death. But instead of allowing fear to lead our discipleship journey, remember that God is not a God of fear but of love. The power in this text comes when we recognize the call to faithfulness, obedience, and the relentless pursuit of discipleship. We are to remember powerful and faithful stories as described in Hebrews 11 (read it!). Much like many faithful and obedient biblical characters who have come before us, we too are called to remain faithful and obedient to Jesus and his teachings. In the space below, journal a prayer that the Holy Spirit (who is the very presence of God, here to empower us to live an obedient and faithful life) would empower you to lead a salty life that brings honor and glory to God.

Study the Story

Read Matthew 5:14.

In the ancient world, light is a common and powerful image used to describe the purpose of the people of God. Read the verses below.

Daniel 12:3

Isaiah 42:6

Isaiah 49:6

Isaiah 51:4

Isaiah 60:3

What do these verses indicate about the impact of light?

Whenever we see the word *nations* in the Old Testament, we can also read it as *Gentiles,* or anyone who is not descended from Abraham's family line (i.e., not Jewish). This understanding gives us insight into the mission of God in the world.

The people of Israel not only long for a new hope to dawn, but they are also considered to be a light to the rest of the world.

Read John 1:1–9; 8:12. The light that the world so desperately needs—both in the ancient world and still today—is fully realized in Jesus Christ. If Jesus is the light of the world and he also calls his disciples light, how does this change our view of a disciple's role in the world?

Think of a community or an individual who best exemplifies being a light to the nations. What kinds of things do they *do*? What kind of *character* do they have?

Jesus uses three different images in Matthew 5:14 to illustrate how light impacts darkness:

"A town built on a hill cannot be hidden."

"Neither do people light a lamp and put it under a bowl."

"Instead they put it on its stand, and it gives light to everyone in the house."

Jesus is clearly concerned with the penetrating impact light has on darkness. Although this might seem like the most basic concept for us today, we often forget the power that light can have in a dark, sinful, broken, and hurting world. Jesus summons his disciples to shine their lights in such a way that the world actually becomes a little bit brighter. If a disciple lives as a *true* disciple, then the disciple's light can't possibly be hidden.

For some, the responsibility of being the light of Jesus might seem daunting. We may be tempted to believe that we have to become the next Mother Teresa. But good works can and do happen in the daily rhythms of our everyday lives. In the space below, list five *intentional* ways you can be a light in your world. (Try to come up with things you are *not* already doing.)

Live the Story

The purpose of a light is none other than to shine and not be hidden. Over the course of the next week, light a candle before bedtime and pray this prayer.

Christ be with me
Christ before me
Christ behind me
Christ inside me
Christ beneath me
Christ above me
Christ on my right
Christ on my left
Christ where I lie
Christ where I sit
Christ where I rise
Christ in the heart of every person who thinks of me
Christ in the mouth of every person who speaks of me
Christ in every eye that sees me
Christ in every ear that hears me
Salvation is of the Lord.*

Optional: Write your own version of this prayer or add your own personal touch to the one above.

*http://www.irishcentral.com/roots/old-irish-prayers-and-blessings-for-you-and-your-family-for-every-occasion-172538071-237790491.html.

Learn the Story
Video Teaching Notes

Salt functions as an ingredient to make something else better. The purpose of a light is to shine and not be hidden.

JESUS IS THE FULFILLMENT OF THE LAW

Read the Story

Matthew 5:17–32

¹⁷ "Do not think that I have come to abolish the Law or the Prophets; I have not come to abolish them but to fulfill them. ¹⁸ For truly I tell you, until heaven and earth disappear, not the smallest letter, not the least stroke of a pen, will by any means disappear from the Law until everything is accomplished. ¹⁹ Therefore anyone who sets aside one of the least of these commands and teaches others accordingly will be called least in the kingdom of heaven, but whoever practices and teaches these commands will be called great in the kingdom of heaven. ²⁰ For I tell you that unless your righteousness surpasses that of the Pharisees and the teachers of the law, you will certainly not enter the kingdom of heaven.

²¹ "You have heard that it was said to the people long ago, 'You shall not murder, and anyone who murders will be subject to judgment.' ²² But I tell you that anyone who is angry with a brother or sister will be subject to judgment. Again, anyone who says to a brother or sister, 'Raca,' is answerable to the court. And anyone who says, 'You fool!' will be in danger of the fire of hell.

²³ "Therefore, if you are offering your gift at the altar and there remember that your brother or sister has something against you, ²⁴ leave your gift there in front of the altar. First go and be reconciled to them; then come and offer your gift.

²⁵ "Settle matters quickly with your adversary who is taking you to court. Do it while you are still together on the way, or your adversary may hand you over to the judge, and the judge may hand you over to the officer, and you may be thrown into prison. ²⁶ Truly I tell you, you will not get out until you have paid the last penny.

²⁷ "You have heard that it was said, 'You shall not commit adultery.' ²⁸ But I tell you that anyone who looks at a woman lustfully has already committed adultery with her in his heart. ²⁹ If your right eye causes you to stumble, gouge it out and throw it away. It is better for you to lose one part of your body than for your whole body to be thrown into hell. ³⁰ And if your right hand causes you to stumble, cut it off and throw it away. It is better for you to lose one part of your body than for your whole body to go into hell.

³¹ "It has been said, 'Anyone who divorces his wife must give her a certificate of divorce.' ³² But I tell you that anyone who divorces his wife, except for sexual immorality, makes her the victim of adultery, and anyone who marries a divorced woman commits adultery."

Study the Story

Read Matthew 5:17.

The audacity! What can Jesus possibly mean when he says he came to *fulfill* the law? This verse might very well be one of the most difficult to understand of Matthew's gospel. We can assume that Jesus is countering a claim that he came to abolish the law and that he's setting the record straight that his mission is, in fact, to *fulfill* the law.

Jesus is the pinnacle of the entire story of God.

Another word for *fulfill* could be *complete*. Jesus is the pinnacle of the entire story of God. He is the center. He came to *complete* the promise God gave to Israel long ago.

The Old Testament is often wrongly viewed as a vehicle that simply didn't work and eventually broke down, and Jesus is viewed as the brand-new vehicle that *replaced* the older vehicle. However, this sort of understanding dismisses the mission of God in the Old Testament that was always leading to its pinnacle—that is, Jesus Christ. It would be better to view the Old Testament not as a vehicle that broke down but, rather, as a vehicle that simply reached its destination.

After Jesus utters the words "fulfill the law," the Old Testament is read differently. Suddenly, Genesis, Exodus, Leviticus, Numbers, Deuteronomy, and on, are read *in light of* Jesus and as *moving toward* Jesus.

We are going to read in tandem some verses that claim a fulfillment in Jesus and their Old Testament parallels. As you read these texts, answer the following questions: How does Jesus *complete* or *fulfill* this Old Testament text? Reading the Old Testament text *in light of* the work Jesus has done, how does this particular passage point *toward* Jesus?

Matthew 1:18–23; Isaiah 7:14

Matthew 2:13–15; Hosea 11:1

Matthew 8:14–17; Isaiah 53:4

Matthew 12:15–21; Isaiah 42:1–4

Matthew 13:13–15; Isaiah 6:9–10

Matthew 27:6–10; Zechariah 11:12–13; Jeremiah 19:1–13; 32:6–9

Matthew 27:12–14, 22–26, 32–44, 59–60; Isaiah 53:5–12

Jesus makes the radical claim that the entire story of God comes to completion in him. Therefore, Jesus is to be the ultimate authority for the disciple's life. Either we allow the teachings of Jesus to shape our lives, or we let his words remain in the background.

Read Matthew 8:1–4.

Now briefly skim Leviticus 13:1–45.

Read Mark 5:21–42.

Now briefly skim Leviticus 15.

Leviticus helps us understand why some of the things Jesus does in the New Testament are so upsetting to the religious leaders. He is boldly breaking the laws they have learned to follow meticulously. What kind of statement do Jesus's actions in these verses make in regard to the law and in regard to the person of Jesus?

The purpose of the Old Testament laws were so the people of God would be set apart—pure and holy—from the rest of the world. When Jesus touches someone with a skin disease, he fulfills the *purpose* (or spirit) of the law, rather than the letter of the law, by becoming what Scot McKnight calls the "contagion of purity." If Jesus, then, is the contagion of purity, what does that say about the state of all who participate in Christ?

When we begin to grasp that the entire story of God reaches its ultimate culmination in Jesus Christ, and when we embrace that Jesus is the fulfillment of the law, a powerful statement is made about Jesus's role in a disciple's life. This important statement is not unique to Matthew 5 and can be found in multiple passages throughout the New Testament.

Read the following passages:
Matthew 7:21–29
Matthew 10:22–32
Matthew 28:18–20
John 14:21–23
Hebrews 3:1–6

What common thread do you notice weaving itself through all these scriptures? How does this thread affect our view of what it means to be a disciple of Jesus today?

There might be some things in your life over the next few weeks that have to die. It might be pride, selfishness, hatred, jealousy, impatience, greed, or something else that God reveals to you. Take a few moments to invite the Holy Spirit to search your heart (see Psalm 139:23) for anything in your life that might need to die. Write a prayer of submission to God, praying that your life would be shaped by the teachings of Jesus. Include in your prayer some words of thanksgiving for the cleansing power of Jesus Christ.

Study the Story

Read Matthew 5:21–25.

This scripture begins the section of the Sermon on the Mount known as the antitheses. This series of antitheses is revealing, piercing, and commanding. Jesus demands more from his followers by pushing them to embody his vision for the new kingdom community; the antitheses are proclamations made for the coming and already present kingdom of God.

As Jesus unrolls the antitheses, he not only digs deep into the Jewish scriptures, but he also expands the scriptures of God's original vision for God's people.

It is helpful, then, to grasp some of the scriptures from which Jesus pulls.
Exodus 20:13
Numbers 35:16–21
Deuteronomy 19:1–13
Genesis 4:1–12

What are some of the words used in these scriptures to describe emotions and thoughts?

Anger can lead to murder, and Jesus immediately makes this connection in his sermon. Jesus, therefore, seeks to dismantle anger in the hearts of his followers.

Psychologists often say anger is a secondary emotion, caused by underlying primary emotions. What emotions could lead to anger?

Read the following passages and note the common theme.
Isaiah 43:25–26
Acts 3:19
1 John 1:9

If God promises to forgive us for our sins, how should we respond to those who have wronged us?

In Matthew 5:23–26, Jesus offers counter behaviors that illustrate the reconciliation that is to happen among the people of God, teaching us that reconciliation, forgiveness, love, grace, and unity are earmarks of the kingdom community.

Take a few moments to be still before the Lord. Close your eyes, quiet your heart, and ask God to reveal anyone in your life with whom you need to seek reconciliation. Write down a way to identify that person (whether the person's name, initials, or a description that only you understand). Then write out a prayer for the Spirit to embolden and empower you to have a critical conversation.

Study the Story

To begin, read Matthew 5:27–30.

For the next antithesis, Jesus deepens the understanding of sexual purity for the people of God. Jesus begins by quoting Exodus 20:14 and Deuteronomy 5:18, but then he redefines adultery by expanding the Jewish scriptures.

Before we can push ahead, let's take a walk through some Old Testament texts on adultery. Read Job 24:15 and Proverbs 30:20.

How do adulterers rationalize their actions according to these verses?

In the very same way that the sinful act of murder begins in the heart with anger, the sinful act of adultery begins in the heart with lust. Let's look at another Old Testament example. Read 2 Samuel 11:1–5. What sparks David's adulterous act?

David knows his act of adultery is a heart matter. Read David's prayer in Psalm 51:1–14. Note especially verse 10. It is likely that you can think of a few times in your life that maybe your heart wasn't so clean. Maybe even right now your heart is clogged with impurities. What cleanses our hearts?

Read the following passages:
Ezekiel 36:25–26
2 Corinthians 3:18
Hebrews 10:22
Titus 3:4–7
1 John 1:9

After reading these passages, what can we conclude?

Take a few moments to rewrite David's prayer from Psalm 51 in your own words. You might also confess any impurities in your heart that are causing you to stumble. Remember, these prayers aren't just words on a paper. God sees your prayer, God loves you, and God delights in your prayers.

The seriousness of sexual sin for the kingdom community is more than apparent in Matthew 5. All too often, sexual sin is kept hidden, and many walk through a sexual struggle alone. But as Christians, we aren't meant to be on this journey alone. There is power in confession, accountability, and corporate prayer, but shame is also powerful, and shame is often what keeps us from reaching out when we need help. What are some helpful actions Christians can take to counter sexual sin in the church without using the power of shame and judgment?

Read Matthew 5:31–32 and then take a deep, deep breath. There is likely someone in your life who has endured a divorce (maybe even you). Let's take a look at some other passages on marriage and divorce.

Deuteronomy 24:1–4
Exodus 21:10–11
1 Corinthians 7:10–11

What differences do you see between the Old Testament passages and the New Testament passages (including the Matthew 5 text)?

Read Matthew 19:1–11.

Is Jesus justifying Mosaic law, or condemning it? Or neither?

What is Jesus's definition of adultery according to verse 9? Why?

It is common practice for us today to seek from the Bible justification for divorce. But if we approach the Bible that way, in any situation, we often miss the entire point. Jesus speaks into a community that has become entirely too relaxed regarding divorce. Once again, Jesus pushes the listeners beyond the known norm and invites them into a new normal for the people of God.

It seems that today's environment is not much different from the one Jesus speaks into. Divorce is commonplace these days. Unfortunately in today's society, love has been limited to just *feelings*. However, love is a *commitment* that we must make *daily*. This love is best exemplified in the love of Christ, who laid down his own life for his friends (John 15:13).

Read Ephesians 5:25–33. Contrast the world's definition of love with the picture of love presented in these verses.

If you are married, write a list of ways you can better love your spouse as Christ loves the church. If you are not married, write a list of ways you can display the love of Christ to the people around you.

Let's face it: Marriage can be difficult, but Jesus is clearly against thoughtless or frivolous divorce. On the other hand, we can't ignore some of the complexities that creep into marriages, such as infidelity or abuse. Things aren't always as black and white as we would like. Like Jesus, we should be *for* marriages that are holy and *against* divorces that are self-seeking, and we should always strive for full understanding, prayer, and discernment in any marital situation. God's grace and love are not out of the reach of divorced people.

Take a moment to read Romans 8:31–39. Read it slowly, maybe a few times. Note the promises in this passage. Allow these promises to penetrate your heart, mind, and soul. Know that God's love does not exclude any person. Take a few moments to write out a prayer to thank God for his all-consuming love for us.

Live the Story

If the Spirit has revealed some brokenness in your life and maybe even darkness in your heart this week, the good news is that we have learned that God's grace, love, and forgiveness are far-reaching and also that God has given us the gift of the Holy Spirit to cleanse our hearts and transform us into God's glorious image. But the process of transformation is a long journey of choosing daily to seek the empowering presence of the Spirit and the daily life of obedience.

One of the ways you can start this journey of transformation is by praying for God to help you overcome specific struggles in your life. Find a piece of string or twine and make a knot in it for each struggle God revealed to you this week. Once you have all your knots tied, place your hand on the first knot and make your way down the row, pausing to talk with God about what each knot represents. Carry the string around with you for the rest of the week and pause to pray down the row of knots throughout each day. If you can't think of any struggles, let your knots represent people in your life whom God can help you love better.

If you need help knowing what to pray, start with this prayer:

Most merciful God,
we confess that we have sinned against you
in thought, word, and deed,
by what we have done,
and by what we have left undone.
We have not loved you with our whole heart;
we have not loved our neighbors as ourselves.
We are truly sorry, and we humbly repent.
For the sake of your Son, Jesus Christ,
have mercy on us and forgive us;
that we may delight in your will,
and walk in your ways,
to the glory of your name.
Amen.*

*Modified from the *Book of Common Prayer.*

Learn the Story
Video Teaching Notes

"...that we may delight in your will,
and walk in your ways."

LOVE YOUR ENEMIES

Read the Story

Matthew 5:33–48

33 "Again, you have heard that it was said to the people long ago, 'Do not break your oath, but fulfill to the Lord the vows you have made.' 34 But I tell you, do not swear an oath at all: either by heaven, for it is God's throne; 35 or by the earth, for it is his footstool; or by Jerusalem, for it is the city of the Great King. 36 And do not swear by your head, for you cannot make even one hair white or black. 37 All you need to say is simply 'Yes' or 'No'; anything beyond this comes from the evil one.

38 "You have heard that it was said, 'Eye for eye, and tooth for tooth.' 39 But I tell you, do not resist an evil person. If anyone slaps you on the right cheek, turn to them the other cheek also. 40 And if anyone wants to sue you and take your shirt, hand over your coat as well. 41 If anyone forces you to go one mile, go with them two miles. 42 Give to the one who asks you, and do not turn away from the one who wants to borrow from you.

But I tell you, love your enemies and pray for those who persecute you, that you may be children of your Father in heaven.

---

43 "You have heard that it was said, 'Love your neighbor and hate your enemy.' 44 But I tell you, love your enemies and pray for those who persecute you, 45 that you may be children of your Father in heaven. He causes his sun to rise on the evil and the good, and sends rain on the righteous and the unrighteous. 46 If you love those who love you, what reward will you get? Are not even the tax collectors doing that? 47 And if you greet only your own people, what are you doing more than others? Do not even pagans do that? 48 Be perfect, therefore, as your heavenly Father is perfect."

Study the Story

At the beginning of the Bible's narrative, dishonesty propelled humanity into the new normal when the serpent distorted God's words in the garden of Eden (see Genesis 3). This new normal for humanity was now tainted with partial truths, dishonest answers, and twisted words.

Read Genesis 12:10–20. How do Abram's actions in this passage reflect the brokenness of humanity's new normal?

Read Genesis 29:1–30. How does this story reflect humanity's brokenness?

Verbal trickery was common in Old Testament narratives.

Now read Matthew 5:33–37 and Deuteronomy 23:21-23. What is the seriousness of not fulfilling a vow?

It was common practice for early Jewish followers to avoid invoking God's name in an oath (for fear of breaking Exodus 20:7) and instead develop a practice called "social swearing."* So, instead of swearing by the name of God, one might swear "by heaven and earth." This is what Jesus is refuting in Matthew 5:34–36. He makes the point that swearing by any of these is not swearing *less*—because heaven and earth are God's anyway.

When a person lies, it is an attempt to control a perception, a person, a situation, or an outcome. But these are not ours to control. Jesus reigns as King, and we live in the new community. What situation can you think of from popular culture, news, or media where a lie was the result of an individual seeking to control something?

_____

*R.T. France, *NICNT Matthew*, 215.

When have you have lied in order to control a situation?

If fulfilling an oath was so important in Old Testament ethic, why does Jesus command his followers to no longer swear an oath?

Jesus's greater ethic is no doubt radical in nature. Take a few moments to reflect on your own life. Does Jesus's ethic push you to recognize much-needed transformation in your life when it comes to truth telling? Write a prayer in the space below asking the Spirit to empower you to die to dishonesty and pursue truth at all cost.

Study the Story

Begin by reading Matthew 5:38–42.

Commensurable punishment is an idea in the court of law that punishments are to be equal to the crime committed. The Latin term for this is *lex talionis*—also known as the law of retribution.

Read the following verses and note the common thread running through them:
Exodus 21:23–25
Leviticus 24:19–20
Deuteronomy 19:21

The principle behind the law of retribution is simple: Justice requires moderated retribution in the hope of curbing violence. Otherwise, violence will spin out of control. Instead of requiring moderated retribution, however, Jesus steps in and does what he's been doing throughout the entire Sermon on the Mount—illustrate how the new kingdom community is to live. Being merciful is not easy, especially in the face of evil. What examples can you think of—either from the news or your personal life—of someone showing mercy when it wasn't deserved?

Read Isaiah 50:6. What is remarkable about this verse?

Read Matthew 26:67–68. Then read Matthew 27:12–14, 27–31. How do these verses show that Jesus meant what he said in Matthew 5?

What is Jesus's posture in the face of evil?

Write about a time when you experienced an injustice and responded with grace, love, mercy, generosity, or kindness.

Study the Story

Begin by reading Matthew 5:43–48.

We are often tempted to interpret the second half of verse 45 as God punishing everyone (including God's own followers) in equal measure. But in the biblical, agriculturally focused society, Jesus's hearers understand that rain and sun are both needed to help their crops grow. So they hear Jesus's words as an assertion that God provides equally for those who do good and those who do not. How does this understanding change how we view Jesus's words and God's provision in Matthew 5:45? Why would God provide good things for bad people?

Jesus points out a unique challenge for believers in verse 46–47. How does Jesus challenge his followers to be different from the world around them?

Read Luke 10:25–37. What might Jesus say *today* if we were to ask the question, "Who is my neighbor?"

The radical call to discipleship is striking in this antithesis. As children in the kingdom community, we are to have a boundary-breaking, indiscriminate, countercultural, cross-cultural love for all. Just as Jesus loves *all* people, we are to love all people. Why is it sometimes a challenge to love *all* people?

In this final antithesis, Jesus introduces a peculiar term, *telios* (perfection). In today's culture, the idea of perfection can seem incredibly daunting. Reread Mark 12:28–31 and Matthew 5:43–48 and let these verses soak into your heart and mind for a few minutes. After reading these passages, answer the following question: When Jesus commands his followers to "be perfect . . . as your heavenly Father is perfect" in Matthew 5:48, what does he mean?

———

Several years ago, while serving as a pastor in a local Nazarene church, I built a relationship with an elderly man in our congregation. "Joe" had an intense desire to study Scripture and was always full of questions on Sundays. One day Joe had a change in perspective. On a Sunday morning, while I was preaching a message, Joe made his way down the center aisle and sat in the front row; I almost expected him to interrupt the sermon.

At the end of the service, Joe was quick to jump up and hand me a sheet of paper with various scriptures written in red ink. "This is the holy Word of God," he said. "I can't argue with God." When I looked down at the paper I noticed that it was filled with passages similar to 1 Timothy 2:12. Joe continued, "Since you are a woman, you have no business preaching and teaching." As I attempted to gently walk Joe through some of the passages, I quickly realized I was getting nowhere as he only got angrier. Joe's words were piercing and left me feeling wounded that day, as I have felt other times after receiving similarly harsh emails, letters, or phone calls from those who oppose my ministry.

Five days later, Joe had a severe brain aneurysm and almost lost his life. As a single man with hardly any family in town, Joe didn't have many people to visit him. Since our other pastor was on vacation, I was on hospital-visit duty. Knowing that our last conversation had left me wounded, I struggled to come to terms with the thought of visiting Joe. As I arrived at the hospital, I stopped for a moment to whisper a prayer. I asked the Spirit to propel and impel me to love Joe with the same, self-sacrificial love of God that Jesus talks about in the Sermon on the Mount.

When I walked into the room, I was overcome with compassion for Joe. I saw him slumped in a wheelchair with his head down, staring sadly at the floor. He was alone and helpless; it hurt my heart. I had never sensed such loneliness and brokenness as when I looked at Joe that day. I sat next to him, and we began to talk. About halfway through our conversation, I placed my hand on his and said, "Joe, we've been praying for you at church, and we love you." As those words came out of my mouth, his body shook with emotion, and he began to weep uncontrollably. And I knew I meant it; I loved Joe. The Spirit had, indeed, propelled and impelled me to love him with the indiscriminate love of the Father.

With the Spirit's help, how can you begin to intentionally turn your enemies into neighbors by showing the love of God? What are some specific examples?

Live the Story

Life has its hardships, especially when it comes to relationships. People say things that hurt us; we say things that hurt others; best friends stop talking over seemingly petty things; even family members can go years without talking over a bad fight. Sometimes just a bad look from another person can send us into a tailspin of insecurity and anger.

This week, we've been sitting with a challenging command from Jesus: It is no longer enough to love our neighbors and hate our enemies; rather, we must now love our enemies *and* pray for those who persecute us. Take a few moments and think about the people in your life who are simply hard to get along with.

Read Luke 6:27–28.

Find a non-permanent marker and then go outside somewhere where rocks can be found.

Meditate on the above verses, and as you do, ponder the names of the people you consider enemies. When a name pops into your head, pick up a stone and write the person's initials on it.

While holding the stone in your hand, say a prayer of blessing for the person whose initials you wrote. After the prayer, wash the stone in water and allow God to wash away the grudge you hold against that person as the water washes off the ink.* Do this as many times as you need for as many enemies as you can think of. Or put all your enemies on one rock and wash them all away together.

Commit to praying for the person or people for the next few days.

---

*Idea taken from *Creative Prayer: A Collection of Contemplative Prayer Stations,* by Faith McCloud (2012).

Learn the Story
Video Teaching Notes

It is no longer enough
to love our neighbors
and hate our enemies;
rather, we must now love
our enemies and pray for
those who persecute us.

PRAYER AND FASTING

Read the Story

Matthew 6:1–18

[1] "Be careful not to practice your righteousness in front of others to be seen by them. If you do, you will have no reward from your Father in heaven.

[2] "So when you give to the needy, do not announce it with trumpets, as the hypocrites do in the synagogues and on the streets, to be honored by others. Truly I tell you, they have received their reward in full. [3] But when you give to the needy, do not let your left hand know what your right hand is doing, [4] so that your giving may be in secret. Then your Father, who sees what is done in secret, will reward you.

[5] "And when you pray, do not be like the hypocrites, for they love to pray standing in the synagogues and on the street corners to be seen by others. Truly I tell you, they have received their reward in full. [6] But when you pray, go into your room, close the door and pray to your Father, who is unseen. Then your Father, who sees what is done in secret, will reward you. [7] And when you pray, do not keep on babbling like pagans, for they think they will be heard because of their many words. [8] Do not be like them, for your Father knows what you need before you ask him.

[9] "This, then, is how you should pray:

"'Our Father in heaven,
hallowed be your name,
[10] your kingdom come,
your will be done,
on earth as it is in heaven.
[11] Give us today our daily bread.
[12] And forgive us our debts,
as we also have forgiven our debtors.
[13] And lead us not into temptation,
but deliver us from the evil one.'

[14] For if you forgive other people when they sin against you, your heavenly Father will also forgive you. [15] But if you do not forgive others their sins, your Father will not forgive your sins.

[16] "When you fast, do not look somber as the hypocrites do, for they disfigure their faces to show others they are fasting. Truly I tell you, they have received their reward in full. [17] But when you fast, put oil on your head and wash your face, [18] so that it will not be obvious to others that you are fasting, but only to your Father, who is unseen; and your Father, who sees what is done in secret, will reward you.

Study the Story

Begin by reading Matthew 6:1–4.

The principle in this passage is clear: *Am I doing my good deeds for God, or am I doing them for others?* Think of a specific activity in your life (such as tithing, teaching a Bible study, serving at a church activity, helping in the community). Write the activity down and then ask yourself introspective questions:

Activity:

Why am I doing this?

Who is watching me? (Think especially about who might see you perform this activity because of the way you draw attention to it on social media.)

What about this activity brings me pleasure?

What actions might Christians engage in that appear selfless on the surface but could have impure motives underneath?

Take a few moments to write out a prayer. Maybe today's prayer needs to focus on asking the Spirit to cleanse your heart of any impure motives; or maybe it's a prayer of gratitude that you get to serve; or maybe you pray that God steers you to use your time, talents, and resources in more meaningful ways.

Why am I doing this? Who is watching me?

Our Father, who art in heaven

Hallowed be thy name.

Thy kingdom come, thy will be done

On earth as it is in heaven.

Give us this day our daily bread,

And forgive us our sins

As we forgive those who sin against us.

And lead us not into temptation,

But deliver us from evil.

For thine is the kingdom and the power and the glory forever.

Amen.

Study the Story

Begin by reading Matthew 6:5–8.

Then read the following Old Testament passages:
Deuteronomy 6:4–9
Deuteronomy 11:13–21
Numbers 15:37–41

These three texts combined make the *Amidah* prayer the Jewish people prayed daily. What do you notice about the content of the prayers?

Read the following scriptures and note the different prayer regulations being followed (such as frequency, time of day, and attitude):
Daniel 6:10
Acts 3:1
Mark 11:25
Luke 18:11–13

These prayers would be prayed first thing in the morning, again in the afternoon, and once more before bed. So even though most were likely to be at home for morning and evening prayers, people could be anywhere for midday prayer. The hypocrites Jesus talks about planned where they would be at the hour of prayer—in a place where others would notice. Jesus's teaching in Matthew 6:5–8 is a reaction against this sort of overt and praise-begging behavior. Many Christians today don't follow a regimented prayer schedule on a daily basis (though certainly there are those who do), but our motives are still important to recognize. What are some ways that Christians today might use prayer as a way to make themselves look good rather than as a way to be transformed by God?

Prayer is an intimate communion that exists between God and God's people, and it is central to the Christian life. Answer this question honestly: How is your prayer life? Think about whether it might be time to come up with a regular rhythm of prayer for yourself. Take a few moments to reflect on your prayer life in the space below.

Study the Story

Read Matthew 6:9–15.

Jesus invites the disciples to engage God in prayer. If prayer is an intimate conversation with God, what does this say about God's desire for God's people?

Verse 9. Calling God "Father" is intimate, no doubt. What attributes of God can we infer from the opening lines of the Lord's Prayer in verse 9?

Verse 10. The word *kingdom* can be complicated in biblical scholarship—there are entire books written on the single word alone! Jesus's intent with that word in verse 10, however, can be summed up with a term biblical scholars like to use—*already, but not yet.* We celebrate the *already* in what King Jesus has done on our behalf, while we long for the future (*not yet* here) kingdom of God to permeate the world. For a simple exercise in trying to grasp some of this, make a list of the things that have *already* been done for us, and make a list of things that have *not yet* been done for us.

Already:

Not Yet (see Revelation 21):

How can Christians begin to live into the future kingdom *now*?

Verse 11. What does this verse communicate about trust in God?

Verses 12–13. Write in your own words your interpretation of these verses.

Make a list of things for which God has forgiven you (especially when you haven't deserved it).

Read the following scriptures:
Matthew 4:1–11
James 1:13
1 Corinthians 10:13

How can these scriptures interpret each other?

What does Jesus's example during his temptation experience communicate to us about how we should endure our own temptations? (Remember, Jesus was *fully human*.)

Verses 14–15. Why is forgiving those who have hurt us (even badly) critical for the people of God?

Read Matthew 6:16–18.

Read the following Old Testament passages and write down the different events, practices, or rituals the fasting mentioned in each of them is connected to:
Leviticus 16:29–31

Leviticus 23:26–32

Psalm 35:11–16

Isaiah 58

Acts 13:1–3

The context into which Jesus speaks about fasting is one in which the practice of fasting has been abused. Read Zechariah 7:5. How does the condemnation of insincere fasting remind you of Christian practices or rituals today that have become insincere?

The purpose of biblical fasting, according to the scriptures we've read, is:

The purpose of biblical fasting, according to the scriptures we've read, is not:

Read Mark 2:18–22. In this passage, fasting is linked with kingdom hope. In light of this passage, when do you think would be an appropriate time to fast?

For Jesus, motive is *critical*. Any time we participate in an act of piety for the sake of drawing attention to ourselves, we do not bring honor to God. What can we learn about the Christian life and acts of piety from what Jesus says about fasting?

Sometimes reciting prayers can become so repetitive that we stop thinking about what we are *actually* praying. Take a few moments to write the Lord's Prayer in the space below, but instead of mindlessly writing it from practiced memory, allow the words to be the very language of your heart to your heavenly Father.

Live the Story

"A prayerless life is one of practical atheism."*

The reality is, we don't pray *enough*. Think for a moment about the frequency of your prayer life. Is it once a day? Once a week? Less?

Find a notecard or small piece of paper. Take some time to be still before the Spirit. Listen. Be quiet. And then, after a while, write out a short prayer on your notecard. Commit to carrying around this notecard for the next seven days and praying this particular prayer three times a day.

If you don't know what kind of prayer to write, consider putting the Lord's Prayer on your notecard.

---

*Gordon D. Fee, *Paul, the Spirit, and the People of God* (Grand Rapids: Baker Academic, 1996), 149.

Session 6

Learn the Story
Video Teaching Notes

Take some time to
be still before
the Spirit.
Listen.
Be quiet.

JUDGMENT AND DISCERNMENT

Read the Story

Matthew 6:19—7:12

¹⁹ "Do not store up for yourselves treasures on earth, where moths and vermin destroy, and where thieves break in and steal. ²⁰ But store up for yourselves treasures in heaven, where moths and vermin do not destroy, and where thieves do not break in and steal. ²¹ For where your treasure is, there your heart will be also.

²² "The eye is the lamp of the body. If your eyes are healthy, your whole body will be full of light. ²³ But if your eyes are unhealthy, your whole body will be full of darkness. If then the light within you is darkness, how great is that darkness!

²⁴ "No one can serve two masters. Either you will hate the one and love the other, or you will be devoted to the one and despise the other. You cannot serve both God and money.

²⁵ "Therefore I tell you, do not worry about your life, what you will eat or drink; or about your body, what you will wear. Is not life more than food, and the body more than clothes? ²⁶ Look at the birds of the air; they do not sow or reap or store away in barns, and yet your heavenly Father feeds them. Are you not much more valuable than they? ²⁷ Can any one of you by worrying add a single hour to your life?

²⁸ "And why do you worry about clothes? See how the flowers of the field grow. They do not labor or spin. ²⁹ Yet I tell you that not even Solomon in all his splendor was dressed like one of these. ³⁰ If that is how God clothes the grass of the field, which is here today and tomorrow is thrown into the fire, will he not much more clothe you—you of little faith? ³¹ So do not worry, saying, 'What shall we eat?' or 'What shall we drink?' or 'What shall we wear?' ³² For the pagans run after all these things, and your heavenly Father knows that you need them. ³³ But seek first his kingdom and his righteousness, and all these things will be given to you as well. ³⁴ Therefore do not worry about tomorrow, for tomorrow will worry about itself. Each day has enough trouble of its own.

(Chapter 7)

[1] "Do not judge, or you too will be judged. [2] For in the same way you judge others, you will be judged, and with the measure you use, it will be measured to you.

[3] "Why do you look at the speck of sawdust in your brother's eye and pay no attention to the plank in your own eye? [4] How can you say to your brother, 'Let me take the speck out of your eye,' when all the time there is a plank in your own eye? [5] You hypocrite, first take the plank out of your own eye, and then you will see clearly to remove the speck from your brother's eye.

[6] "Do not give dogs what is sacred; do not throw your pearls to pigs. If you do, they may trample them under their feet, and turn and tear you to pieces.

[7] "Ask and it will be given to you; seek and you will find; knock and the door will be opened to you. [8] For everyone who asks receives; the one who seeks finds; and to the one who knocks, the door will be opened.

[9] "Which of you, if your son asks for bread, will give him a stone? [10] Or if he asks for a fish, will give him a snake? [11] If you, then, though you are evil, know how to give good gifts to your children, how much more will your Father in heaven give good gifts to those who ask him! [12] So in everything, do to others what you would have them do to you, for this sums up the Law and the Prophets."

Study the Story

Read Matthew 6:19–24.

How do verses 22–23 relate back to verses 19–21?

How does verse 24 relate back to verses 19–21?

How are verses 19–24 about more than just possessions and money?

Read James 5:1–6. How does James expand on the kingdom vision of Jesus?

Read the following passages and answer this question: How are these passages similar to Matthew 6:19–24?

Psalm 39:6
Ecclesiastes 5:13–17
Luke 12:13–21

1 Corinthians 7:29–31
James 1:10–11

Read the following verses and answer this question: How is the heart connected to a person's possessions, treasures, and desires?

Matthew 5:8
Matthew 11:29
Matthew 12:34

Matthew 15:18–19
Matthew 22:37

Read Luke 14:33. Why does this verse make us uncomfortable?

Read Matthew 6:25–34.

Read the following passages:
Exodus 16
2 Kings 4:42–44

What do these two stories tell us about God's provision?

Read Matthew 14:13–21.

How does Jesus's character reflect God the Father's character in the Exodus and 2 Kings passages?

We must keep in mind that Jesus is talking to disciples who are living in the context of itinerant ministry and who have no other choice but to trust in God's daily provision as they minister along the dusty roads with Jesus. But at the same time, Jesus demands that his disciples get their priorities straight—and so must we.

Read Matthew 6:25.

Be still for a moment.

What has you worried?

Read Matthew 6:26–30. What does Jesus call those who are unwilling to trust the hand of God for the necessities of life?

Read verses 31–32. What does it mean to trust that God knows what we need?

Read verse 33. How do we seek God's kingdom and righteousness?

What does it mean that "all these things" will be given to us if we seek God's kingdom first? All what things? What will it look like?

Read verse 34.

Jesus's sayings on possessions are so clear that it's almost disturbing. Jesus is calling his disciples to a single-minded focus on the kingdom of God. We are *supposed* to be rattled, uncomfortable, and challenged while reading these passages.

My husband, Jeff, and I bought our first home while I was pregnant with our son Caleb. It was my dream house, and I could not *wait* to have a place to call my own. I'll never forget what our real estate agent said to us when she handed over the keys to our brand new house: "I'll see you again in about five years when you buy your next house!"

Next house? Was our beautiful, 1700-square-foot, three-bedroom house not enough? Would we someday be bored with our home and long for bigger and better?

And I did. I did long for bigger and better. With two rambunctious boys, toy cars and trucks have taken over our home. Legos and superheroes are replacing my once beloved candles and decorations. There have been many days I've thought, *If only we had a basement or more storage for our stuff.* There have been days that I've spent way too much time on Realtor.com lusting over bigger homes. And there have been times when I've spent way too much energy imagining Jeff or myself driving around in nicer cars.

In Matthew 6, Jesus beautifully commands us to store up a single treasure, live with a single vision, obey a single master, and seek a single goal.

So Jeff and I have had to ask ourselves: *What does it mean to seek first the kingdom of God? Are our dreams made up of the desire for bigger and better? More stuff? Bigger houses, nicer cars, better toys, and granite countertops?* I am certain that when Jesus said, "Seek first the kingdom of God," he did not mean seek first bigger houses. What if he does have something bigger and better but not in the way some might imagine?

Again, we have asked ourselves: *What if we step into the kingdom vision instead of the typical American dream? What if we refuse to live the status quo just because it's what the family down the street is doing?*

To be single-minded about our treasures, our visions, and our Master, we must pursue first the kingdom of God. A single-minded kingdom vision is letting God do the dreaming for us and recklessly abandoning our own. It's tapping into the wild, untamed imagination of our King.

Take a few moments and write a few paragraphs on what this might look like for your own life. How would your life need to be reoriented to have a single-minded focus on the kingdom of God instead of our earthly possessions?

Write a prayer. Maybe you want to confess your inappropriate attitude, or maybe you want to pray for the Spirit to help turn your heart to God in everything you do. Take a few moments and ask the Spirit to reveal to you where your heart is. Write your thoughts to God.

Study the Story

Read Matthew 7:1–5.

Why is it important not to judge? (Go beyond quoting verse 2.)

Write about a time when you have projected your own shortcomings onto someone else.

What might be a modern-day example of a plank in our eyes?

Read James 4:11–12. What do these verses say about our role as humans?

Read 2 Samuel 12:1–14. What is the difficult lesson David learns in this text?

Scot McKnight writes, "We must learn to distinguish moral discernment from personal condemnation. This distinction—the ability to know what is good from what is bad and to be able to discern the difference versus the posture of condemning another person—enables us to see what Jesus prohibits in this passage [in Matthew 7]."*

---

*Scot McKnight, *The Story of God Bible Commentary: Sermon on the Mount* (Grand Rapids: Zondervan, 2013), 227.

What is the difference between judgment and discernment? Think about current events in the last couple of years. What is an unhealthy example of judgment from Christians and a healthy example of discernment?

Read John 8:1–11. Describe the posture Jesus takes toward the woman.

Take a few moments to reflect on your posture toward sinful people in this world. In the space below, write a prayer asking for the Spirit to produce love, patience, kindness, grace, and generosity in your life. (Read Galatians 5:22–23 if you need a reminder of this promise!)

Study the Story

Read Matthew 7:6. What is your initial reaction after reading this verse?

Read Matthew 13:45–46. How does reading these verses change how you read Matthew 7:6?

Read Matthew 10:14. Jesus is giving his disciples these instructions in the context of them spreading the gospel.

If the gospel is sacred, what or who might be the pigs and dogs referenced in Matthew 7:6?

If the gospel is sacred, how do we know when to share it?

Knowing when to speak up and when to be silent takes discernment and wisdom from the Spirit. When have you seen or taken part in a proclamation of the gospel that honored God?

When have you seen or experienced a proclamation of the gospel that did not honor God?

Read Matthew 7:7–11.

Then read Proverbs 8:17 and Jeremiah 29:13–14.

How are the promises in all three of these passages conditional?

Read James 1:5–6 and James 4:3.

How do these passages expand on the teaching of Jesus in Matthew 7:7–11?

Read Matthew 26:39. How does Jesus get what he asks for in this prayer? Why does he not get *everything* he asks for?

Whether we realize it or not, we anchor our prayers in God's character. Read the following verses and write the character of God described in each verse:

Psalm 37:4

Psalm 84:11

Isaiah 49:15

Read the following verses:

James 1:16–17

Matthew 7:11

Luke 11:13

If we believe that God is good, how does that change the way we pray?

Describe a few examples of why we might become discouraged in prayer.

When our prayers seem to go unanswered or are not answered in the way we desire, how should we respond?

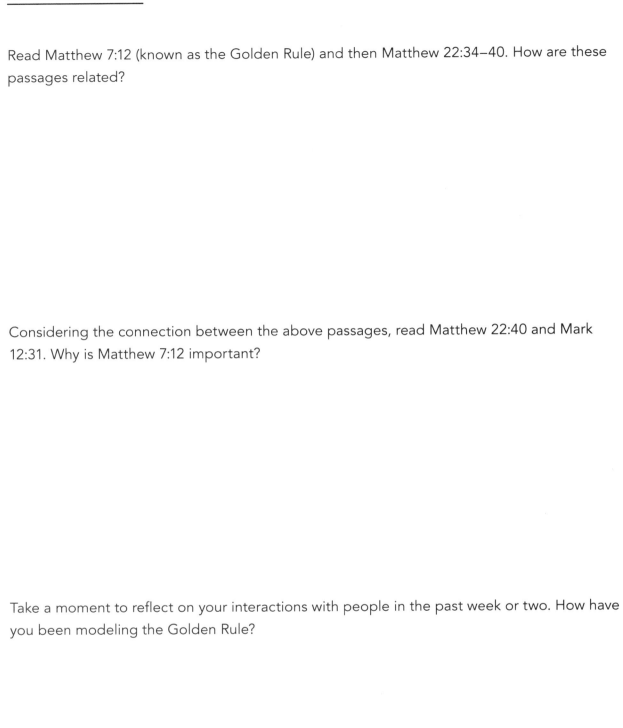

Read Matthew 7:12 (known as the Golden Rule) and then Matthew 22:34–40. How are these passages related?

Considering the connection between the above passages, read Matthew 22:40 and Mark 12:31. Why is Matthew 7:12 important?

Take a moment to reflect on your interactions with people in the past week or two. How have you been modeling the Golden Rule?

In the space below, write a prayer thanking God for his goodness and for the good gifts that have been given to you. Pray also that the Spirit would empower you to live and treat others with love, grace, and goodness.

Live the Story

The breath prayer is a spiritual discipline that has been practiced for centuries by our church ancestors. Using our breath to help us focus and meditate on God, the breath prayer concentrates on one thought, one image, one concept that, in turn, fastens us on God. This contemplative prayer form can be used not only in our daily routine and prayer life but also during times of anxiety, fear, distress, frustration, or illness. The breath prayer can be said comfortably, strengthening us to keep our focus on God in a regenerated spirit.

Get into a comfortable position, whether on your knees, sitting, lying down, or standing.

Ask God to calm your mind and heart.

Slow your breathing and think about the rhythm of your breath.

Repeat your breath prayer silently in whatever rhythm is most natural with your regular breathing.

As you breathe in, acknowledge who God is or a character trait that describes God.

As you breathe out, make your request.

For example:
[breathe in]
Lord Jesus Christ, Son of God
[breathe out]
Have mercy on me, a sinner

Another example:
[breathe in]
God of peace
[breathe out]
bring me comfort

Continue repeating this prayer with every breath you take for a minimum of one minute, up to five minutes.*

---

*Adapted from *Creative Prayer: A Collection of Contemplative Prayer Stations*, by Faith McCloud (2012).

Learn the Story
Video Teaching Notes

Lord Jesus Christ,
Son of God
Have mercy on me,
a sinner
God of peace
Bring me comfort

DISCIPLESHIP AND THE WISE & FOOLISH BUILDERS

Read the Story

Matthew 7:13–27

13 "Enter through the narrow gate. For wide is the gate and broad is the road that leads to destruction, and many enter through it. 14 But small is the gate and narrow the road that leads to life, and only a few find it.

15 "Watch out for false prophets. They come to you in sheep's clothing, but inwardly they are ferocious wolves. 16 By their fruit you will recognize them. Do people pick grapes from thornbushes, or figs from thistles? 17 Likewise, every good tree bears good fruit, but a bad tree bears bad fruit. 18 A good tree cannot bear bad fruit, and a bad tree cannot bear good fruit. 19 Every tree that does not bear good fruit is cut down and thrown into the fire. 20 Thus, by their fruit you will recognize them.

21 "Not everyone who says to me, 'Lord, Lord,' will enter the kingdom of heaven, but only the one who does the will of my Father who is in heaven. 22 Many will say to me on that day, 'Lord, Lord, did we not prophesy in your name and in your name drive out demons and in your name perform many miracles?' 23 Then I will tell them plainly, 'I never knew you. Away from me, you evildoers!'

24 "Therefore everyone who hears these words of mine and puts them into practice is like a wise man who built his house on the rock. 25 The rain came down, the streams rose, and the winds blew and beat against that house; yet it did not fall, because it had its foundation on the rock. 26 But everyone who hears these words of mine and does not put them into practice is like a foolish man who built his house on sand. 27 The rain came down, the streams rose, and the winds blew and beat against that house, and it fell with a great crash."

Study the Story

Read Matthew 7:13–14.

Why would the gate be narrow?

Read Deuteronomy 26:16–19.

Throughout the history of Scripture, there is a noticeable pattern that emerges from the big story: Obedience is mandatory for the people of God. Jesus wants his listeners to reflect on their lives and remember that how they choose to live *actually matters*. Disciples are faced with a daily choice: Follow Jesus, or don't follow Jesus.

Take some time to reflect on our study thus far. Maybe even flip through your homework, your notes, and Matthew 5—7.

Make a list of as many things as you can that Jesus demands a disciple of his to do.

Attempting to live out the demands of discipleship without being connected to Jesus would be futile. How is your connection to Jesus? Take a few moments to invite God's grace, presence, and power to empower you to live out the kingdom vision illustrated by Jesus. Write your prayer in the space below.

Study the Story

Read Matthew 7:15–23.

What is a false prophet?

What is the type of deceit Jesus warns against in verses 21–23?

Read Matthew 3:10.

How can we come away from these verses with hope rather than fear?

Read the following texts:
1 Corinthians 12:1–3
1 John 4:1–3

How can you detect whether someone is living by the Spirit?

Many of us reading these passages may wonder, *Am I in or out?* We might even be wondering if the good fruits Jesus has in mind are visible in ourselves. We must be willing to ask ourselves whether we exhibit the behaviors expected of a follower of Jesus. Day-to-day, simple acts of love are required.

Think about the various leaders you've encountered in your life. Think about ones who exemplify day-to-day, simple acts of love on a regular basis. Who are they? How do they exemplify the love of God? What fruits emerge from their lives?

Study the Story

Read Matthew 7:24–27.

How does Jesus's analogy play out in real-life terms? How can we be wise and avoid being foolish beyond what verse 24 says? What does it mean to put Jesus's words into practice in our lives today?

Read Ezekiel 33:30–33. What warning is implied in verse 33?

Read James 1:22–25. How does James expand on the teachings of Jesus?

The Sermon on the Mount calls the disciples of Jesus to live out the kingdom vision by a life of radical obedience. Of course, we are faced with a choice: To follow or not to follow? To obey or not to obey?

Take a few moments to reflect on all of the commands of Jesus that we have read in this study. What do you choose? In the space below, write an honest prayer to God about your response to the teachings of Jesus. Take your time on this prayer; be thoughtful; be honest.

Live the Story

It's time to share.

You've been on an incredible journey of learning and growing and formation these last few weeks. Think of a friend, family member, coworker, neighbor, or someone else in your life with whom you could share what you've learned. Think of someone who hasn't been in this study with you, invite that person to coffee, and ask if you can share about all that God has done in your life over the last several weeks of this study. Think of someone who is *ready* to hear this testimony and will be encouraged by your story. Take your time thinking of a name. Pray about it and ask for the Spirit to lay a person's name on your heart.

Learn the Story
Video Teaching Notes

"Therefore everyone who
hears these words of mine
and puts them
into practice is like a
wise man who built his
house on the rock."
—Matthew 7:24